# *SENSUOUS and SULTRY:* SEX IS FOR THE COURAGEOUS

By: Paulette Tomasson

**Dedicated to Angoro and Suzanne Kyra**

*"When your sexuality is healthy, it permeates every aspect of your well-being."*

- Suzanne Kyra

## Disclaimer

This book is based on the opinions of the author and is <u>not</u> a substitute for therapy. Given the nature of the material contained therein, a reaction to the content may be forthcoming. If so, the reader is advised to stop reading and seek professional assistance immediately.

Sensuous and Sultry: Sex is for the Courageous
By: Paulette Tomasson © 2014
Editor: Margaret Tucker MA, RCC

# Table of Contents

# Introduction

I wrote this book for several reasons: firstly to ignite in you a desire to embrace the full potential of your sexuality and secondly, to offer you my forty years experience as a nurse clinical counsellor in private practice. I have seen first hand the pain and suffering that misinformation and misuse of sexuality brings to so many lives and the destruction can be profound. I have also seen people journey through their hurt and pain to reconnect to their sexual innocence and joy.

I believe our sexuality is a wonderful, rich aspect of our humanity. My passion is to see people embrace and revel in it in a healthy empowering way. I want you to be informed so that you can be enriched by your sexuality and embrace its vitality and joy.

Sexuality has many aspects: it is one of the most vulnerable and empowering parts of who we are. It can be exhilarating and rewarding, as well as painful and disheartening. Your relationship with your sexuality requires sensitivity, awareness and nurturing. In today's society it is very easy to get caught up in the hype of media expectations which may lead you to question your connection and beliefs. What is healthy? Am I a prude or am I over-sexed? Am I normal? It is more important today to be sensitive to your own rhythm and flow, your own needs and desires, than it was in the past.

Misinformation and misuse of sexuality abounds in our culture and is often very confusing. Thus, it can be difficult to find deep meaning and connection in any of it. Our curiosity, without valid information, can lead us to areas that will exhilarate or harm us. How do we trust our instincts without more information? How do we navigate through the multiple mazes to find what fits for us?

This is not a book about techniques of intercourse or how to find a mate as there are many wonderful books on the bookshelves and online today. This is a book about what sexuality is at its very core and ultimate levels. In this discussion, we will explore the exciting primary aspects of sex, the six types and also the journey required to embrace the true sensuous and sultry joy of it.

I trust this book gives you the information you require to help you begin your journey. I encourage and invite you to dive into this exploration with curiosity and courage. If you wish to, answer the questions thoughtfully and keep a journal of the changes you may feel. This can be a wonderful adventure. I will describe to you an empowered, fulfilling and joyful connection to your sexuality.

Paulette Tomasson
Registered Nurse
Registered Clinical Counsellor
Bachelor of Science in Nursing
Master of Arts in Counselling Psychology
Certified Sex Addiction Therapist-Supervisor

# Chapter 1: Sex. What Is It Anyway?

I am a therapist. I grew up in a tiny hamlet in rural central Canada. Life on the prairies was raw, real and remarkable. Natural world sexuality was vibrant and nature surrounded you with it in its purest form. How the males strutted their colours and stature in the hope of attracting and being chosen by the female of their species with no sense of shame. How proud they were to be male. Courting was an art form with no sense of timidity or embarrassment. The female would rebuff the advances until the one she deemed worthy of her attention appeared. Many games were played, demonstration, push and shove until the mating. It appeared so simple and biological. Absolute, innate honesty. How refreshing and definitely not the method that is promoted to humans today. Instead information abounds with instructions on how to manipulate and entrap. How sad it is that love and sex have been decompensated to this level. How sad that the beauty of courtship has been lost.

The dictionary defines sex in two ways:

As a noun: 'sexual activity, including specifically sexual intercourse.'
As a verb: 'to attempt to arouse sexually.'

I am a firm believer that sex is much more than either of these two definitions. In my opinion sex is the underlying essence of who you are. Sexuality is reflected in your passion: passion about what you love, passion about what you do and passion about who you are. You know how it feels to be in the presence of someone who loves who they are and is excited about what they do. They are alive, engaging and you feel more alive and excited by just being with them. It is contagious. They ignite vibrancy in you, causing you to feel more awake and aware. This is sexuality at its best: it is passionate aliveness, vibrant and utterly unashamed.

Are you connected to your passion? How do you express it? Are you aware that it is your passion you are expressing? Sometimes we are expressing our passion and we are totally unaware of what we are doing. Then someone mentions how they see us come alive when we are talking about it, or how they like being with us when we are engaged in that particular activity and we are almost shocked. Are you excited about your life? Are you passionate about who you are and what you do? Do you ask yourself why?

When we are connected to our sexuality, in the true essence of ourselves, we embrace it in our bodies, our minds and our souls. We like being male or female: we express our joy of it in the way we dress, in the way we walk and in the way we interact with others. We are juicy living beings. We treat our bodies with respect and honour, we feed ourselves healthy food, we get enough exercise and we make sure we have enough sleep and rest. We understand the importance of love, sensuality and sexuality.

We fill our minds with good intellectual information and pleasurable experiences and thoughts. We laugh and play. We nurture our spirit and connect to the mystery of life. All of this feeds our sexuality, our sensuality and our sense of being a human being in our bodies. This is a passionate sexual life.

## Chapter 2: Gender Specific

Our gender is the essence of our embodied sexuality. It is the pure expression of our masculinity or our femininity. History has placed many limitations on the expression of maleness and femaleness. There were, and are, very distinctive lines regarding what each gender is allowed to do and how they are to behave. Can little boys play with dolls, other than GI Joe, and not be ridiculed? Can little girls play with trucks and have it be okay? Some people are attracted to the same gender. Others may feel trapped in the wrong body. They know they were not born in the right body and embark on a long journey to have their bodies reflect their inner spirit and true gender. Some feel ashamed of their gender and the stereotype that is connected to it. Many have not had their bodies respected and were abused. Some hate their bodies while others are obsessed with thinking they are perfect specimens: another form of self-loathing. None of us can be graded as imperfect or perfect.

There are so many different stories, so many different beliefs, myths and ideas about what is normal and healthy. And it is important to remember that normal doesn't necessarily mean healthy. In fact it just means that the majority of us fall into that aspect of the bell curve. For instance, normal blood pressure today is higher than the healthy number and normal of the past, possibly due to the added salt in our food. There are many theories as to why. Therefore normal blood pressure is not really that healthy anymore. The pure expression of who we are is the combination of our mind, body and spirit.

- As a man, when you think about yourself and your sexuality what do you feel?
- How do you stand proud in your maleness?
- How do you not?
- How do you strut your maleness with real confidence?
- How do you strut your maleness without an inflated ego or with aggression?
- How do you compete with a sense of honour for both yourself and your opponent?
- How do you not?
- How do you show up and show your interest in the person of your choice with clean pure intent?
- How do you not?
- How do you accept their acceptance or decline with dignity?

- How do you not?
- What are your values around sexuality? List them.
- How are you gentle, sensitive and humble as well as strong and powerful?
- How are you not?
- How do you appreciate the feminine and honour her as an equal?
- How do you not?
- How do you suffer from male entitlement?

The answers to these questions are all essential attributes to establishing healthy male sexuality. A strong healthy male is proud to be a man and honours his feelings. He knows all of his assets and also is fully aware of his liabilities. He is in charge of his testosterone, it does not rule him. In this way he is safe for a woman or a man to be with him in a relationship. Sadly, this is not always what our society values nor models. Sometimes the opposite is insisted upon and sexuality becomes a political power game with power over being the goal. And the power over is usually over anything that is different. And sometimes that is the feminine.

The female has a different experience in the world regarding her sexuality. She has a complicated expression and her sense of pride is different from the masculine. Feminine sexuality is not so much expressed in physical strength as it is in physical sensuality. It is this very sensuality that has brought about fear in herself and the male when not valued. For centuries women have been revered and punished for their intuitiveness and ability to know. Their sensuousness was seen, at times, as seductive and evil and some of the remnants of that are still evident today.

- As a woman can you be soft, strong and confident in being imperfect?
- How do you honour your femininity?
- How do you not?
- How do you respect your intuition, your feelings and sensitivity?
- How do you not?
- How do you use your femininity to defend yourself?
- How do you not?
- How do you trust your knowingness?
- How do you not?
- How do you get caught up in self-doubt?
- How do you not?
- How do you treat yourself with respect and hold your truth?
- How do you not?
- How do you honour other women?
- How do you not?
- How do you have health competition with other women?
- How do you not?

- How do you honour your body and treat it as your temple?
- How do you not?
- How do you criticize your body and focus on its imperfections?
- How do you not?
- How do you use your body or allow it to be used in a dishonouring way?
- When do you not?
- When do you overfeed it or starve it or overwork it?
- When do you know and own your sexual power and express it with dignity?
- When do you not?
- When do you use your body and sexuality to seduce and get your way?
- When do you not?
- How do you respect the cycles of your body and embrace the deeper rich meaning of them with a sense of awe and wonder?
- How do you not?
- Can you grasp the amazing essence of the feminine and its power to create, the actual deep spirituality of the feminine?
- How do you appreciate the richness of its gifts of feeling, intuition, creativity, knowingness, intelligence, connectedness, strength, power, courage, caring, tenderness, tending, love, joy and so much more?
- How do you educate yourself about the feminine?

- Can you embrace these and not get caught up in the degrading of the feminine that has happened throughout the ages?
- How do you shrink from your power because of fears that you will be labeled as a '_itch' or abandoned or shamed?

Society still struggles with accepting powerful women. Many cultures keep their women shrouded and unseen.

- How does this affect you?
- Can you hold your power as the male comes forward and struts his intent to court you or does not notice you?
- When do you get overwhelmed and shrink or cave?
- When might you let go of your power and collapse into the belief that you need to accept a man's attention and somehow you are privileged to have it?

It is a woman's natural instinct to move towards a man. She needs to be aware of this and be in charge of her self so as not to have this instinct on automatic. She needs to use her intuition and good sense to make sure the man is safe, deserving and a good fit to be with. Many relationships have begun in unconscious instinct - without conscious choice and the couple is left wondering what happened. Where did it all go wrong? When conscious choice is utilized, the relationship has a greater chance of lasting and flourishing.

Our awareness of our gender along with its assets and liabilities is part of the great journey of life. Most struggles are due to the lack of fully understanding our sexual path.

In Western society there are few, if any, rites of passage for men or women to honour the true essence of the genders. Because of this, we lack anchoring rituals that link a deep connectedness to the core of our maleness or femaleness. This causes us to flounder in our attempt to find our way. We get lost in the media and other's exploitation of our sensitivities and take on harmful beliefs and actions that damage our true sexual expression. Only when we embrace and honour our masculinity or femininity will we experience the true and clear passion and joy of our sexuality.

## Chapter 3: The 6 Types of Sex

When I tell my clients that there are six types of sex, their ears perk up and I know I definitely have their attention. So are you ready? Here they are with an explanation of each.

#1 Pro-creational sex

This is sexual intercourse for the specific purpose of impregnation. Most often we associate this type with couples executing their desire to have a baby, to start a family or increase the family size. However, this isn't always the case. Throughout history, this type of sex was not as loving and pure in its intent. It has been used to procure an heir to the family farm or the throne. Marauding armies raped the women of their conquered lands to spread their DNA and quell the numbers of the possible resistance in the future. This type of sex is for the continuance of the human race. It is essential for humanity and it is sometimes magical and sometimes not pleasant at all.

# #2 Recreational Sex

This type of sex is for fun. It is considered playful and has been described as bodies on bodies having a good time. This type of sex requires a playful spirit. It is full of laughter and games and here is where our childlike innocence and imagination reign. It is where fantasy can come to life, the French maid, the handsome cowboy, etc. With two people engaged in having fun it can be pure joy with laughter. For this to work the partners must feel completely safe, trusting and open.

However, it can become complicated when commitment becomes an issue. It is important to note that most women cannot engage in recreational sex for any length of time without a commitment. Her experience of sex is different than a man's and in order to feel safe, she will need to know the relationship is moving towards something more.

This type of sex is most easily accessible in the beginning of the relationship due to the flow of hormones. Early in a relationship our serotonin levels drop and our androgens increase and thus we are more excitable and less inhibited.

# #3 Relational Sex

This is more commonly known as making love and here intimacy, deep passion and love reign. This is where one also demonstrates deep caring, vulnerability and a willingness to be cherished by another. This is love making in a deep, connected openness and it's the reason songs are written and novels are penned. This is love personified and sexual passion does not fade when relational sex is practiced. In this type of sex, passion actually increases. It is pure, honest and connected. Feelings are expressed, honoured and partners are loved.

# #4 Spiritual Sex

Spiritual sex is commonly called Tantra. Tantric sex is deep and devotional. It is experienced and practiced in order to connect to the essence of your spirituality. It is a meditative ritual to enhance one's connection to the self, the partner and one's own spiritual essence. This type of sex is an ancient practice from an Eastern philosophical basis and requires teaching by a Tantric master. To practice Tantra, one needs discipline and commitment for this is a deep process that not everyone is willing to explore. Those who do report an experience close to ecstasy.

## #5 Energetic Sex

This is that electrical charge that races through your body with certain people. It is what people call chemistry But what is chemistry? I'm so glad you asked! Well, chemistry is the release of certain neurochemicals and sex hormones (androgens) when we see a specific person that completely fits our arousal template. This is different from general attraction as we can be attracted to many different people. We can like certain body types, certain hair colour, etc. but chemistry is different. This particular connection sends chemicals rushing through our brains and causes us to almost become obsessed.

This type of sex is hot and lustful. There is an energetic connection that travels across and through all barriers and people can sense their partner on opposite sides of the earth. They know when they are in trouble and they can sense when they have stepped outside of this energetic field. This is more than intuition, it is akin to what Rupert Sheldrake calls "morphic resonance". There is an energetic pull that can, at times, be exciting, beautiful and it can lead people to feel crazy. The sexual connection with this type of sex can be intoxicating and can become almost addictive. And at other times it can be very painful, depending on the circumstances.

However it does not have to be. If the person is grounded and aware, they can embody this wonderfully powerful chemistry and have it connect to their passion. When grounded, it can help to energize their lives in a very powerful way.

Do you have the grounding to be able to stay centered in this chemical reaction and not loose your bearings? Can you channel this energy into your passion for life? Can you be in charge of it rather than it being in charge of you? Everyone has experienced this chemistry at one time or another in his or her life. Some have been able to use it wisely and develop a long lasting relationship full of passion, while others have succumbed to losing their power and falling into the painful addictive side of this beautiful experience.

#6 Compulsive Sex

This type of sex is known as the destroyer. It destroys relationships, families and individuals. This sex is based solely on self-centered need: the need for a certain behavior, a certain frequency, a certain look, a sound, a movement, or a certain situation in order to feel aroused. It requires a lack of connection to the partner except as a tool to satisfy the need. This sex is based on power to have the need met and usually fuelled by fear and shame. The scene can be a scene that must be re-enacted in a specific way to heighten the arousal and climax. There is no enhancing of or connection to the partner for anything other than self-satisfaction. The rituals and fantasies are power and fear based. Partners may be degraded and shamed. Connection to humanity is minimal if at all. This type of sex is lustful and intense and is based on disconnection. It is harmful to both participants. There is no joy.

The first five types of sex can all be experienced in a healthy relationship, which can bring joy, passion and connection. However if you participate in the sixth you will be courting destruction. Ultimately this will lead to disconnection, discontent and dissolution of the self and the relationship.

## Chapter 4: Vows and Curses

What are vows and curses and what do they have to do with our sexuality? Most of us understand vows as promises we make to another person and the most familiar ones are wedding vows that couples make in front of their loved ones. Vows are powerful and supposed to last forever. However we make vows to ourselves as well and these are the ones we need to explore regarding our sexuality. How many times have we limited our lives because of a vow we made when we were hurt many years ago?

Vows and curses have very powerful influences on how we see ourselves and how we conduct our lives. Vows commit us to follow through forever and sometimes we don't even remember what the vow was or when or why we made it. Most vows that affect our sexuality are made under the influence of very intense emotions. The usual suspects are hurt, anger, shame and fear. These are not the emotions of clarity and rational thinking. Instead, they are the emotions of reaction and impulse. It is essential, when uncovering our beliefs regarding our sexuality, that we take a good long look at old vows that may be restricting us.

Is there an outdated belief or vow that is holding us back from sexual freedom? Did someone hurt us or shame us, and in that intense moment, did we vow to never be vulnerable again? Did we vow to get even no matter the consequences? Did we believe it was our fault and start to shut down our passion? These vows can lead to behaviour that diminishes our sexual freedom.

Curses on the other hand are verbal incantations placed on us by others. Remember the wicked witches in fairy tales? They placed curses on people they wanted to disempower. In our modern world, we don't have witches to do that for us any more so we use our own words to attempt to do the same thing. We say nasty things to people directly or indirectly through others and when we do that we are attempting to disempower them. If the person believes what we say, even a little, the word will have an affect. Just like the old, the target person is disempowered. How many times have we limited our own lives because of a vow we made when we were hurt many years ago?

Curses are the words spoken to you in an attempt to disempower you regarding your sexuality. If the words are impactful and there is even a very small part of you that can believe them, they will stick. They will stick to you like a black veil over your sexuality and your sense of self. The danger is when we embrace the curse and the voice becomes our own. These words are really verbal sexual abuse. Remember the intent of the person was to disempower and possibly shame you. What does that tell you about them? How self-assured is someone who would do that? How insecure would they need to be in their own sexuality? Think about it as you reflect on these questions.

So how can you uncover these vows and curses and is it possible to rid yourself of both? Why yes, it is absolutely possible to remove the influence of both. Awareness is the beginning and the most basic part and so you need to ask yourself these questions.

- What is the foundation my sexual knowledge is based upon?
- How sound is this foundation?
- Is there anywhere in my connection to my sexuality that feels restricted?
- How long have I felt this?
- What was happening when I first felt this?
- Did I react and make a vow at that time?
- If I did how do I view the situation now?
- Do I still need to feel that restriction?
- How does it serve me to keep it?

- Have I done it long enough?
- Can I forgive the younger more vulnerable me for imposing the vow on me?

The process to rid yourself of the curses someone has placed on you is very similar.

- Is something others have said that keeps you from experiencing the joy of your essence?
- What did they say?
- Was there a part of you that believed it was true?
- Do you still believe it?

If you do, then you might want to get some help in doing some deeper work around it. If not, are you ready to let it go and shake off those words and stand tall in your own truth and beauty. And again, can the older wiser you of today forgive the younger you of yesteryear for taking on the curse? It is my hope that you can.

Vows and curses are powerful and can influence our sexuality. They restrict and limit our ability to experience the joy of being a truly fully embodied sexual being.

## Chapter 5: Self–disclosure Versus Over–exposure

With the explosion in social media, the ability to communicate and share images has never been so easy. Pictures and videos abound; the ability to snap, click and send in an instant has a powerful impact on many of us. Today, it is not just celebrities who are having their lives exposed to the world without permission. Now we are all subject to the possibility on a daily basis. Our anonymity is rapidly being lost and privacy is becoming a thing of the past.

We can have a false sense of safety as we are encouraged to expose ourselves more and more on a daily basis. Facebook, Twitter, Instagram and others rely on us to provide our pictures and information in order to run their companies. These are not bad companies, but we are the ones who need to be aware and sensitive to what information we are putting out into the world. Many of us are not aware of the boundaries or what they are. In addition, there is texting and sexting. We may think it's private but one slip of the thumb and it goes out to someone else or everyone. Oops – and now you can't undo it. There is no recall button.

- What do you feel comfortable sharing about yourself?
- Are you sure you want that picture going around the web?
- If your relationship ends, do you trust your partner not to spread those pictures?
- You might think it's funny or cute today, but what about tomorrow?
- Would you want your parents or children to see it?

Sometimes in our desire to belong, to be part of, we expose ourselves more than is necessary and definitely more than we are really comfortable. Some questions to ask yourself in regards to this are:

- Am I really comfortable with anyone or everyone knowing or seeing this about me?
- Do I really want to share my sexuality in this way?

If there is any twitch or the slightest doubt, don't do it. Instead take time to decide and do not be impulsive about this. A decision to not go ahead today may be greeted with a deep sigh of relief tomorrow.

The sharing of ourselves is a very personal and private matter. If we open ourselves up more than we are comfortable or ready to do, it will cause us to feel shame. If you feel embarrassed you have over-exposed yourself. If someone else has shared things about you that you don't want out in the public domain, you will feel over-exposed and betrayed. Your vulnerability is a gift that you share with those who will respect it and keep you safe. Too many young people today are over-exposed and believe that is just how things are, just the way of life. As a result, they have nowhere to feel safe. I find that very sad. This over-exposure has caused such pain for some and has led to dire consequences for others. This is the dark side of social media.

When we are ready to share parts of ourselves, we will feel open and will share from our strength. How will you know what to share? It can be confusing so check in with yourself. Does this feel safe? Do I want to share this? If yes, then we won't feel shame. We will feel connected and resourced. We won't feel diminished and regretful. That is self-disclosure. It is a choice and is a well-grounded decision.

Many of us may need help in developing our boundaries. In todays' culture it can be confusing as it seems that everyone is doing it and we question our reservations. Check in with yourself and if the answer doesn't seem to be clear, ask a wiser, trusted person. Take care of yourself and only share what you feel ready, open and willing to. You decide what you want people to know about you, no one else has the right to tell your story, it's yours and yours alone.

Save yourself from embarrassment and regret. Save your vulnerability for the people who love and value you. It is a gift you are giving when you share. Giver beware!

## Chapter 6: Grace, Courage & Curiosity. The Adventure Begins

So how do we get to this joyful, open, sensual and sultry sexuality? How do we connect to our true spirit and sexuality? Do you really want to know? Do you have doubts that it is even possible?

Of course you do, after all many of us do to some extent. The process begins with reaching down deep inside to connect with your courage, as it is there you will find the answer. If it is yes, then it is very possible.

This journey is one of discovery and reclaiming. Let yourself be curious, allow yourself to wonder. What you will uncover are the real gems of who you are - your uniqueness and your passion. There are many things about yourself and your beliefs that will be revealed. Do you wonder what they will be? Many of us are afraid of what we will find, afraid some of the beliefs we have harboured might be true. These are very common fears and they are usually false. In my counselling practice, the most common thing people discover underneath all the fear and hurt is innocence and joy. It is fear that holds us hostage and prevents us from claiming our passion. Whatever beliefs are discovered, you will keep what is true and the false you will let go. Because of the sensitivity of this journey, I believe it is essential to work with a qualified therapist who has the knowledge, expertise and experience to help guide you through your discovery process, especially if there is a history of sexual abuse or exploitation. Support is always a good thing to have.

This journey requires courage, curiosity and reflection. It is a complete exploration of your early discoveries and experiences around your sexuality. It is the journey of growth and development in learning about what it feels like to be a man or a woman.

- What were the expectations of you as a young girl or boy?
- Were there role distinctions in your upbringing?
- Were you treated differently, and if so what were those differences?
- Were they expressed openly or were they subtle and sensed but never verbalized?
- What did your father teach you about being a boy or a girl?
- What did he actually say or what was it implied?

- How did he treat your mother?
- Were you allowed more freedom if you were a boy than if you were a girl?
- If so what message did that give to you about yourself, your power?
- What effect did it have on your view of the other sex?
- What did your mother teach you about being a woman or a man?
- What did she model in regards to her femininity?
- Did she treat herself with respect?
- Did she insist that others treated her with respect?
- How did she treat your father and the men in her life?
- What did her behaviour towards them teach you in regards to being a woman or how to treat a woman?

So much of how we view ourselves as a man or woman is learned in our families. It is important that a good review of those days be undertaken. This is the foundation of our sexual development and attitudes towards our sexuality. It is the basic knowledge required in order to understand our beliefs. And is the only way to connect with our true choice and our true sexuality. Even if you have little to no memories of your sexual development it is still possible to review and gain knowledge. Be curious. This can be a real adventure and remember it is not a journey for the faint of heart.

I invite you to begin ongoing journaling. It is a great way to explore the past so you can protect your future. Again, this is a journey for the courageous. Let courage and curiosity be your guides throughout your journey. I can assure you the rewards will be more than worth it.

Reclaim your birthright!

## Chapter 7: Introductory Exercises To Sensuous & Sultry Sex Discovery and/or Recovery

These exercises are a great beginning to your journey. Be gentle with yourself and your body. Don't rush it, take time to allow your body to respond and give you the information required for deep healthy connection.

### Your Personal Exploration

Exercise 1: Sit quietly in your favorite spot and breathe gently

Notice your body. Where do you feel strongest? Where do you feel tension? Notice. Where do you feel relaxed? Be curious with your body. Notice without judgment and continue to breathe gently.

Explore your body, sensing the rhythm of your breath, sensing the sensations. What are you smelling? Remember your favorite fragrance. Is it the odor of fresh brewed coffee or the smell of the ocean or the air after a summer rain?

- What are you seeing (if your eyes are open)?
- What colours?
- What colours even if your eyes are closed?
- Remember your favorite site. Was it a sunset or the beauty of your favourite flower?

What is the taste in your mouth? Remember the taste of your favorite food, the first bite into a fresh ripe apple, or the taste of your favorite ice cream. Notice what happens in your body as you remember these tastes.

- Now notice what are you hearing?
- Can you hear your breath?
- What are the sounds around you?
- Or are you noticing the silence?
- What is the sound of silence like for you?
- Remember your favorite sound. Was it the sound of children laughing? Was it the sound of the surf crashing against the shore? Was it the symphony or the aria in the opera? Notice your body as you remember.

What are you noticing on your skin? Are you feeling the warmth or the coolness of the air?

Remember your favorite touch. Was it touching soft plush cotton sheets or the silky feel of fresh flower petals? What feels pleasant and pleasing to your skin? Do you prefer a warm sudsy bath to a hot shower?

Notice how your body feels as you work through these different sensations. Be aware of what nurtures your body and your sensations. This is a great way to begin your sensuous journey.

Allow yourself at least 10 minutes to do this as you begin. You can take more time as you feel more comfortable. Be sure to journal about your experience.

Exercise 2: Gather many different genres of music on a play list

Make sure you have enough space to move freely and safely as your eyes may be closed part of this exercise. Begin with your favorite song or music. Close your eyes and notice your body.

- What happens as the music begins?
- Where do you first notice your body's response?
- Does your body respond?

If you are sitting allow your body to move as it wants to. It may want to continue to sit or it may want to get up and move. Continue to follow the flow of your body to the music. As the music changes to different genres be aware of the differences in your body as it does. Notice if there is more freedom of movement with one type of music or another.

- Is there more aliveness with one type of music or another?
- What music brings your body joy?
- What music causes it to close off?
- What music energizes you?
- What music allows you to feel sensuous?
- What happens when the music is sultry?
- Does it arouse you?
- How does that feel?
- Can you revel in the energy?

Notice and become aware.

Allow yourself at least 10 minutes of this or more if you have the time. Do this a couple of times a week. It is a great way to connect with your body and your passion.

Again, journal about your experience.

Exercise 3: Touch

Skin is the largest organ in the body. It is highly sensitive and can give us great pleasure. It is both a barrier and the organ of contact with the outside world. The more sensitivity connection we have with our skin, the more pleasure we can enjoy.

Gather together some fragrant oils, a silk scarf, a fresh flower or flower petals and a feather or anything that you love to touch. Then laying naked on your bed apply the oils to your skin. Start slowly and gently, noticing the sensations.

- Which parts of your body like to be touched?
- Which parts do not?
- Which parts want a softer touch?
- Which parts want a firmer touch?
- Which parts start to feel aroused?
- Which ones don't?

Notice what sensations come up when you use the feather, or the flower, or the silk scarf? Be very gentle with yourself. If at any time you begin to feel uncomfortable be sure to stop. It may be an indication that you have been triggered and, if so, you need to seek outside help. This is a very good way to explore and find your erogenous zones. Are you aware of yours? This exercise will help you to discover or recover them.

Allow 20 minutes to begin and then more as you become accustomed to it.
Again journal about your experience.

**Your Partnered Experience**

If you have a partner and they have accepted your invitation to join you, here are three exercises for partners. They may seem similar to the exercises for your personal experience, but a partner always raises the energy. Decide who is going to go first.

Whoever it is will be partner A. The other will be partner B. These exercises are by invitation only and need to stop immediately if and when either partner feels uncomfortable. These are to be safe explorations not endurance tests. They are designed to bring awareness and stimulation for more pleasurable sensation and sensuousness. They are for that purpose only.

Exercise 1: Hand Sensation Exercise

Sitting quietly with your partner close your eyes and breathe gently. Notice your body and allow yourselves to get into a relaxed state. Open your eyes and connect to your partner. Partner A reaches out their hand and with one or two fingers begins to slowly and gently explore the hand of partner B. Noticing how B's skin feels to the touch. Partner A notices if there are differences in the sensations in different parts of the hand. After a few minutes of this Partner A then shifts his/her focus to what does his/her finger feel as it moves over Partner B's skin? Notice again the differences.

Partner B during this time is noticing how her/his hand feels being touched in the gentle and slow manner.

- What happens for him/her as Partner A moves over different parts?

- Does it feel comfortable?
- Would Partner B like less or more pressure?
- How does Partner B feel about asking for that?
- If Partner B does, how does Partner A respond?

This is a great exercise for sensing and sharing what is happening during contact. It is a great way for learning more about your own sensuality and your partners. After 5 minutes or more reverse roles and have Partner B be the explorer and Partner A have their hand explored. Share what it was like for you in each role. Which one do you prefer and why. Listen carefully to your partners' experience.

Journal your discoveries.

Exercise 2: Moving Together

Create a play list of different genres in music with each song or score only a minute and a half long. Make sure you have enough space to move and allow 30 minutes for this exercise.

Partner A begins and closes his/her eyes and begins to allow their body to move with the music, noticing the subtle changes as the changes genres.

What music feels sultry? What music feels sensuous? How do you feel knowing your partner is observing you? Allow your body to really express the music. After several pieces open your eyes. Notice if that shift changes your sensations. Partner B watches and notices what music and which movements of Partner A causes them to feel aroused and/or sensuous. Share your experience and change roles.

After both partners have danced for each other do the movements to the music together with eyes closed and then open. Noticing your body and its response.

Share your experience.

Journal.

Exercise 3: Share Your Romantic Fantasies With Each Other

At least once a month take the time to develop an evening where the ambience supports one partners' fantasy. Alternate months.

## Chapter 8: And Let's Continue

Sensuous sultry sexuality is in our essence and our DNA. As previously stated it is our birthright. When we clear away the influences that no longer work that were handed down from our families, imposed by our culture and taken on during our experiences, we will be greeted by our true healthy sexual beingness. It will encompass many facets, and like a well-cut diamond it will shine and reflect out to the world the brilliance of who we are. We will feel it, we will embrace it, and we will luxuriate in it.

If we have the courage and willingness to go on this journey of care and discovery to uncover the essence, we will be empowered and rewarded in a way that may be unimaginable today.

I wish you an alive, honouring, adventurous exploration and an enriched sensuous and sultry connection with your sexuality. And there is more to come ;)

— Paulette Tomasson

# Upcoming Books By Paulette Tomasson

## Sensuous and Sultry: The 6 Types Of Sex

More than a description of the 6 types of sex, this book will take you on an adventure of discovery and exploration of the dynamics of your sexual connectedness. Through questions designed to deepen awareness and exercises to enhance the expression of your sexual being, you will continue your own personal journey of sensuous and sultry sexuality.

## Sensuous and Sultry: Marriage, Is It A Trap?

Why do so many marriages lead to sexual routine and boredom? Can anything be done about that? I believe that sexual passion can actually increase as the relationship ages. This book will look at the primary ways partners disengage in relationship and how to avoid the usual traps that take relationships to the sexual cemetery. In this book you will find the road map for the journey to reignite the sensuous and sultry passion.